THE "L-MODEL" OF LEADERSHIP

A CONCISE METHOD TO ACHIEVE EFFECTIVE LEADERSHIP

CHARLES AYDEN

Copyright © 2019 All Rights Reserved.

No part of this publication may be reproduced, distributed, or transmitted in any form or by any means, including photocopying, recording, or other electronic or mechanical methods, or by any information storage and retrieval system without the prior written permission of the publisher, except in the case of very brief quotations embodied in critical reviews and certain other noncommercial uses permitted by copyright law.

CONTENTS

Introduction 2

Chapter One: Identify 5

Chapter Two: Recruit 10

Chapter Three: Patent 16

Chapter Four: Listen 21

Chapter Five: Separate...27

Chapter Six: Evaluate 36

Chapter Seven: Repeat...41

Conclusion: 42

This is dedicated to my wife and our precious children.

INTRODUCTION

Leadership is defined in a myriad of books and articles, but they all fall short at succinctly explaining how it can best be achieved. Few public organizations successfully identify, foster, teach and promote leadership. To remain competitive, today's private corporations are recognizing the importance of identifying tomorrow's leaders early in the employment lifecycle, how change management is applied, and strategically placing talent in areas reflective of their strengths.

Executive level leaders must find ways to grow their businesses both internally and externally across global markets. Mid-level leadership is equally important and helps steer quarterly goals to align with the overall mission strategy. Line level employees must remain productive and motivated to move the products and/or services at a rate far above satisfactory.

Training and educating employees comes at a cost, either on the front end or the back, which can result in time away from operations and negatively impact profit margins. By providing a concise detailed method, coined the "L Model," that both educates and outlines a proven path to understanding how to become an effective leader, I have opened the doors for entrepreneurs, established business men and women, public servants, and those seeking self-development to become and develop into successful leaders.

Leadership is defined as being the ability to provide direction to a group of people, and influence those people to follow the direction and act accordingly. The "L Model" delivers the concept of leadership in the simplest form and provides a clear understanding of the steps needed for effective leadership.

The "L Model" will test how you identify leadership, and explain how that impacts your ability to become a strong leader. It looks at the importance of bringing in new and developing in-place talent to drive your objectives. American author John C. Maxwell said that "teamwork makes the dream work," but building that team and putting the right components together is in many ways more important than the team itself.

The framework of a team is the roots to its growth. Effective leaders establish and sustain a work culture around them that routinely meets a higher level of productivity than their competitors. They take time to engage their team members, open their minds to new ideas, actively listen, and apply information they receive towards their decisions. These decisions motivate their teams to move in a direction that helps accomplish overarching goals.

The "L Model" walks through how great leaders separate themselves and their organizations from others, by making adjustments to areas that allow them and those around them to be more effective, which in turn promotes positive change throughout the entire organization. After separating themselves from their peers and competitors, successful leaders evaluate and manage change. They communicate to their teams clearly and ensure processes and procedures are aligned with the company's goals and objectives.

The "L-Model" is ideal because it is easy to follow and provides simple, but definitive steps on how to become an effective leader. Let's begin with Step one.

CHAPTER ONE: IDENTIFY

Great leaders are fair, lead by example, earn the trust of others, communicate effectively, give credit to their teams, find ways to overcome difficulties, inspire those around them, exhibit patience and resilience, and make tough decisions. In order to be an effective leader you must first recognize what leadership looks like to you. Because people view leadership differently, the best way to relate to it is to see it and acknowledge it in the form that makes the most sense to you.

My father provided me with a clear vision of leadership. He has always been my role model. He showed me how a leader performs as a dad, as a boss, and as a friend. At home he often said, "when it's time to work, work, and when it's time to play, play." That phrase was a constant reminder to me and my sister to focus on our homework and house chores with the same intensity as we did sports and playing with our friends.

At work my father used a democratic management style. He listened intently to those around him before making hard decisions. He often reminded me to make sure I gathered as much information as possible, given time constraints, before making decisions. As I grow older I see my friendship with my father growing stronger. We share more in common now, and I am able to relate more to the decisions he and my mother had to make when I was younger.

As my friend, my father is my sounding board and we exchange and discuss ideas. I always know he will give me constructive advice no matter the situation. As a result, I have learned to recognize the separation between experience, knowledge and wisdom. I first identified leadership through my father.

Reflect on those who positively impacted your life or others. These people may be parents, friends, teachers, coaches, colleagues, supervisors, community leaders or others. Focus on how they inspired and motivated those around them to accomplish a task or reach a goal. If multiple people come to mind, that's even better. What actions or words did they provide that helped you or others move forward? What were their strengths and how did they handle challenges? Identify these traits and how they delivered on them. Label their style of leadership (i.e. democratic, strategic, laissez-faire, etc…), and think about how they gained your respect. Let those reflections be your guide to understanding leadership.

If you are unable to identify someone who has done this, then ask your close friends and/or family members who they identify as being strong leaders. Research their paths and apply the above questions in an attempt to recognize why they are viewed in that light. Determine how these individuals used their roles to effect change.

Historically, great leaders are passionate about their cause and direction. That passion often drives them to make decisions that promote confidence in others and helps them overcome challenges. Two prime examples of leaders who exhibited these traits are Martin Luther King, Jr. and Mahatma Gandhi. Their charismatic ability to lead by example instilled motivation in their followers.

Today more than ever leaders recognize the importance of having their teams buy into their overall strategy and vision. Corporate leaders such as Ulta Beauty CEO Mary Dillon, Microsoft CEO Satya Nadella, and Alorica CEO Andy Lee are great examples and have successfully led their companies by understanding both their markets and their workforce.

Identifying strong leaders, what they have accomplished, and how they became successful will help mold your leadership qualities and style. It is equally imperative you identify a consistent work ethic and possess character traits indicative of the team you aspire to work with. Below are six tools you can quickly apply to better yourself and help develop your leadership foundation.

1) Self-Assessment: Examine yourself and define your character. What skills do you hold? What are your personal strengths and weaknesses? What two things can you change about yourself that would make you better? Be honest, compile a list, constructively review and implement the necessary changes.

2) Invest: There are few investments worth more than investing in yourself. Whether it is education, time, training or a calculated risk, make the investment if you deem the reward is equal to or greater than the risk. Trust and believe in your own abilities.

3) Set Goals: Prior to starting a project, task or initiative clearly identify your goal. Document your plan from the onset to completion. The plan should outline the shortest way between two points, with contingencies in case things change along the way. Be realistic and implement a reasonable timeline.

4) Commit: Go forward like you are all in. Commit to your goal, and do not let yourself down. Apply the time necessary to complete the task. Frank Ocean said that "excuses are tools of the incompetent, those who use them seldom amount to more than mountains of nothingness." Do not

make excuses, take responsibility and commit to your actions.

5) Be Flexible: Life is a journey and unexpected challenges will present themselves at inopportune times. Be flexible and ready to adjust. Time taken out to wonder what 'could have', 'should have', or 'would have' happened is a waste. Instead, expect the unexpected and move smartly around new obstacles with a re-adjusted plan.

6) Innovate: Never settle on your current position. Continue your self-assessment and engage in behaviors that add value. Know that stagnation restricts growth and innovation provides fuel for positive change.

Apply these tools and identify what leadership looks like through your eyes. This will create a reference point for you to use, as you develop into a successful leader.

Now you are ready for Step two.

CHAPTER TWO: RECRUIT

Strong leaders surround themselves with smart and talented people. Look at some of the best college and professional sports coaches and you will see talented athletes alongside of them. This is no accident. They each take a tremendous amount of time and resources to identify prospective players for their programs.

Successful businesses do the same thing. Placing talent in key positions, coupled with effective leadership, can significantly increase productivity and dramatically impact overall performance. Poor recruitment will lead to the status quo and possibly worse.

Many people get talent confused with experience. Although experience can be an important element, talent is multi-faceted. Look for talent in those with experience and those with potential. Individuals who have a proven expertise in a specific area can bring an immediate return on investment (ROI).

Likewise, talented individuals with less experience, but who display potential can also provide an ROI and be more effective in the long run. They may require more training and an initial investment, but their talents can bring innovation and growth on the flip side. Recruiting these types of candidates who express the fire to learn, eagerness to take on a new challenge, possess solid organizational skills, and integrity can yield a high return on a small risk.

I highlight organizational skills because lacking that trait can be the Achilles heel for even the most qualified candidates. Ideally, you would want a balance of both types of talented individuals (experienced and potential) on your team.

Ensure each candidate's work ethic meets your vision. For many organizations, this can be accomplished by asking behavioral based questions during the interview process. These types of questions give you the best feedback to accurately assess future productivity and work ethic. Prior to bringing new talent onboard review and confirm their references and past work histories. Some organizations outsource employment background checks without adequately reviewing the procedures in place to confirm these important areas. Trust, but always verify.

Be quick to recognize your weaknesses and recruit individuals who can help you turn them into strengths. Remember, you do not have to be an expert in all areas. You simply have to recognize areas in which you need expertise.

After you acquire talent, evaluate it and focus on its correct placement. Occasionally in college football we see the Heisman Memorial Trophy winner go unselected in the National Football League (NFL) draft. How can an individual with so much talent not be chosen to play at the next level? The reason is simple. The player's talent level at that position in college does not equate to success at that same position in the NFL.

Professional scouts and recruiters make that assessment and often try to persuade the player to switch positions, in an attempt to leverage their talent in another area. Rarely are these athletes able to succeed at a new position playing at a higher level of competition.

That example also translates to placing talent at the right levels within the right departments and programs. Additionally, just because an individual is highly productive at the line level does not mean they will be an effective manager. Make sure your organization is prepared for these transitions. Implement a leadership development program for those seeking promotions and include training in the critical areas outlined in the "L-Model of Leadership." Evaluate talent prior to promotions and assign an internal mentor to those selected to help them succeed.

Effective leaders groom talent and initiate succession planning early on. This not only benefits the individual, but best prepares you and your organization for contingencies.

Position your team according to their strengths to give them the best opportunities to succeed. That in turn will put you in an ideal position to make well-informed decisions and lead effectively.

Recognizing individuals with talent, potential, and being able to motivate those individuals to reach their optimum level of productivity is paramount to success. Effective leaders motivate and elevate talent. Although very few leaders can do it consistently, there is great value in accomplishing it even once.

An example of two leaders who have mastered this art are Mike Krzyzewski and Pat Summitt. Both are among the list of the winningest college basketball coaches of all-time. Similar to winning sports programs, businesses will find that recruiting top-tier level talent becomes easier when your program brand equates to success. Prospective players and employees seek successful organizations or programs that breed potential for growth and advancement.

Below are five techniques to help you better recruit talent.

1) Narrow the target: Be specific in your job description not only on the type of position you need, but define a specific skill-set. This will help eliminate poor candidates. Be picky, but do not overlook potential talent. Allow candidates to interview who meet the target, but may lack the experience. You will be surprised at your options. You are looking for desire and passion. Be

prepared to invest in individuals you identify as strong "potential" candidates and develop them by placing them in positions that allow for growth. Consider them alternative investments.

2) Speed up your hiring process: When bringing in new talent ensure your on-boarding process is streamlined. The stages of hiring are the candidate's first glimpse at the inter-workings of your organization. Unnecessary delays can result in losing potential all-stars. For private sector companies anything over 28-days is too long. The job market is unforgiving and candidate pools are not long-term rest stops for those with outstanding talent.

3) Look internally: Do not assume your answer does not lie within your organization. Assess current employees to determine if you can foster or train existing talent to fill a new gap or void. Consider consolidating a position in the department or section you pull from, if applicable.

4) Video record interviews: Conduct at least one interview of each candidate using a video recorder. Prior to making your final decision review the video with at least one manager from a different department who was not a part of the initial interview. Discuss feedback. This allows

for a second unbiased opinion and may help solidify final selection decisions.

5) Fully utilize social media: Millennials and Generation Z candidates are changing the way Human Resource departments do business. Gone are the days where the bulk of recruiting expenses are put into career fairs and magazine advertisements. Strong and persistent social media campaigns are a must. Make sure your company has an established online presence. Recruit on various platforms across several forums. Be creative and construct messaging that best appeals to your target candidates.

Here is Step three.

CHAPTER THREE: PATENT

Once you have recruited and properly seeded talent around you the next step is to patent behavior that meets your expectations. This is where you set the tone for success. You do this by establishing a baseline of performance that matches your expectations. Key areas to patent behaviors are: 1) work ethic, 2) integrity, 3) organization skills, 4) accountability, and 5) efficiency. Each of these areas must align with your overall mission/strategy. Model the behavior you expect your teams to perform at to achieve their goals.

For example, I had a prior supervisor who would begin his workday at 5:30 A.M. each morning. Every time he saw me come in at 7:15 A.M., which was my contracted start time, he walked by my desk and sarcastically said "good afternoon." After hearing that a few times, I quickly adjusted my work schedule and was sure to be at my desk no later than 6:15 A.M.

My supervisor never made that comment to me again, but had set the tone on the importance of getting an early start. Before long each person on our team began coming in earlier and work productivity increased as a result of the extra hours worked. That stuck with me and ever since then I have made it a point to get into the office early. I later mirrored that technique to set the work ethic tone for my team members/direct reports. I also found it increased productivity.

Setting the tone involves physically and verbally letting your team know how you expect things to be done. In other words, you tell people what you expect from them and you hold them accountable. It establishes the culture and provides clarity. This is not micro-management and it does not require a bad attitude. It is simply implementation by practicing what you are preaching.

If visual representation is important, then you should wear business attire and express the importance. If meeting deadlines ahead of schedule are a must, then you show and/or articulate examples on exactly how that is being consistently accomplished. If communication is key to ensure appropriate team members and management are kept informed, articulate how that is done and provide examples (i.e. presentation formats, email distribution lists, phone trees, etc...) to clarify what achievement in that area looks like. The easiest way to eliminate confusion is to clearly articulate your expectations, and maintain accountability to those responsible for meeting them. Pairing new employees/team members with their peers who are already onboard is another excellent way to reinforce expectations.

Some leaders make the mistake of placing more importance on carrying a friendship with their team members than they do in being their leader. In the short-term the friendship will increase morale and bring companionship. However, eventually that will erode when tough decisions need to be made that involve coaching, directing and/or holding members accountable.

For example, an individual was promoted to Team Manager (TM) with 12 direct reports. Two of the direct reports had a longer tenure than the TM and more experience in their department. The TM had shared a close friendship with both individuals prior to the TM's promotion. For the first three months things were going well. The team formed a bond and projects were met within the deadlines.

Shortly after the TM began to realize the two individuals remained good friends with the TM, but were clearly not carrying their weight in the office. Instead of directly addressing this with the two individuals, the TM picked up their slack. A few months later the burden of the extra work hit a breaking point and the TM spoke with the two individuals about their lack of productivity.

Their friendships soon dissolved, and the office culture became almost toxic. Other team members became keenly aware of the problem between the TM and their two co-workers, and the overall morale in the office decreased significantly. The TM was unable to regain the lost friendships and eventually re-established morale with the team after several months. During that time one of the two individuals voluntarily transferred to another department. The individual who remained ultimately increased their work ethic, but never fully re-established their friendship with the TM.

This story is a reminder of what the consequences can be if friendships are placed in front of leadership. Be thoughtful and strategic in how you manage and lead friends. Make sure you clearly articulate your expectations fairly to your entire team, and hold them equally accountable for their duties. True friends will respect your leadership and work hard to help you and their team succeed.

Below are five behaviors that can be used to help you "patent" a successful work environment.

1) Be a coach: Leaders praise openly and coach privately. Provide guidance and develop your team members to meet their full potential. Set challenges against the strengths of your employees. Listen to their concerns and deliver teachable points through examples.

2) Recognize and reward hard work: Call-out the owners of achievements and worthy projects in front of their peers. Make it a point to recognize

employees on their employment anniversaries and birthdays. Praise team members and leaders in a timely manner who go beyond expectations.

3) Make tough decisions: Do not delegate key decisions, make them. Gather as much information as possible, ask questions, and seek opinions from those you trust most before announcing tough decisions. In the end, right or wrong, the fact that you made a decision holds its own weight. Mediocre leaders often fail to step up when needed most.

4) Be empathetic: Do not insulate yourself from the culture of the line level employees. Understand the challenges they face, along with mid-level managers and be cognizant of their feelings. This awareness can help guide decisions and promote directional leadership.

5) Over communicate: Just because you and your executive leadership team know the full background behind a significant change does not mean that others have a clue. Cascade key messages at various levels through multiple platforms. Better to over communicate than underestimate the message reached its recipients. Information is power and providing reasoning during instability will help rebalance employee morale and productivity.

Next is Step four.

CHAPTER FOUR: LISTEN

Effective leaders actively listen and ask questions before drawing conclusions or making decisions. The art of listening is under-valued and significantly under-utilized. Active listening goes beyond simply hearing what a person is saying. It requires your full concentration and the use of techniques to help the listener remember what is being transmitted, as well as, convey confirmation to the speaker their point has been understood.

Leaders who apply this gain valuable insight and are best suited to make decisions. From the onset, take advantage of meeting your team members by learning about their background and perceptions of the organization from on-boarding to present. Ensure your organization's on-boarding program has a place for leaders to engage new hires, even if only via video teleconference. Showing a genuine interest in your employees' opinions can pay dividends down the road and help build rapport. Rapport is the gateway to earning mutual trust. Mutual trust is needed to convince or persuade a person to voluntarily change their behavior.

An experienced crisis negotiator will tell you one of the single most important things they can achieve, short of saving lives, is to build rapport with the individual in crisis. Without rapport your ability to influence or change a person's behavior is significantly more difficult.

I once asked a colleague why is it that when my older sister calls me with a problem and I provide her with a solution, she rarely takes my advice. I began to feel powerless when it came to helping my own sibling in need. I will always remember my colleague's answer. He said, "The reason you cannot change her behavior is because it's personal for you. Instead of using the chronological steps involved with active listening you are going right into problem solving."

He was right. Using active listening with people you just met and those you have established relationships with holds equal value. Needless to say, going forward I made it a point to take his advice and apply it to my future conversations with my sister. It helped tremendously.

For those unfamiliar with the techniques behind actively listening I would encourage you to start with mirroring. Mirroring is simply a way to show the person you are speaking with that you are aligned. This is done through your words and your body language. At various points during your conversation reflect the speaker's message by briefly paraphrasing what they have told you. This confirms your understanding and allows the speaker to continue to talk. It also helps to label their emotions, if you can comfortably identify them.

Emotion labeling is telling the speaker exactly how you perceive what they are feeling. It confirms you empathize with them by quickly being able to understand how the situation they are telling you about has made them feel. Couple this with casually mirroring their body language. With practice and a smooth application, it can feel like a verbal dance.

Your dialogue with your senior managers should be routine and open. This is important and helps foster a "speak truth to power" environment. Surrounding yourselves with a team that speaks truth to power is critical. Even with the best intentions leaders can find themselves in a world where very few people will tell them 'no' or say to them 'I think there is a better way.'

This is very prevalent in the entertainment business, and often has a tragic effect on career paths and financial gain in the end. To avoid this culture creeping into your organization schedule routine meetings with your executive and senior managers, and make it a point to remind them of the importance of speaking truth to power and expressing their own ideas. This practice will leverage your team's knowledge and experience and deepen your ability to solve complex problems.

The "L-Model" of Leadership

In addition to your executive/senior managers, make it a point to engage with employees at various other levels. During my father's time as an executive leader, I had the opportunity to work for him. Every morning he made it a part of his routine to walk around the office and talk with employees at various levels. He referred to these as "walk-abouts." The majority of those conversations appeared to be small talk; however, he consistently accomplished five important things.

First, he subconsciously reminded employees at all levels that the boss is engaging and accessible to everyone.

Secondly, he used those brief conversations to build rapport and develop mutual trust.

Thirdly, he actively listened and learned what was going on in the trenches. This is information you cannot always get at management levels.

Fourth, he personally acknowledged employees' accomplishments and thanked them for their hard work.

Lastly, he set the tone for wearing business attire and maintaining a friendly work environment.

He used the feedback and information that he learned to help him make decisions. This type of leadership technique cannot be used within all companies due to expanded workforce environments, but if feasible it is very effective. Engagement at all levels helps you acquire an "on the ground" perspective that is nearly impossible to replicate from an executive management level.

Below are six tips to help you resolve a problem through active listening.

1) Ask open-ended questions: For example, "tell me how this occurred"? Listen to their response and allow them to tell you their story without interruption. Evaluate the information provided. Refrain from problem solving and ask additional open-ended questions until you have a full understanding.

2) Use minimal encouragers: For example, "ok" or "I see." Simple replies that allow the speaker to know you are listening, but enables them to continue talking. Apply these to extend the speaker's comments and allow yourself more time to learn the details of their issue.

3) Paraphrase: During a pause, succinctly rephrase the content the speaker provided to illustrate your understanding. Once they comply allow them to continue their story. This helps confirm clarity

and allows the speaker to articulate additional details that may provide greater context.

4) Label emotions: For example, "you sound devastated" or "you sound frustrated." By correctly identifying how the speaker is feeling you confirm your understanding of their inner emotions. This holds more value than understanding the content and together it can help quicken rapport building. If multiple emotions exist, label each of them at different times during the conversation. This is an opportunity to express empathy to convey your unique ability to not only understand, but later provide guidance.

5) Summarize: Once you have a full understanding of their problem and have successfully identified their emotions, summarize their entire situation and prepare the speaker for your assessment. Your summary should be brief, but detailed resembling a succinct regurgitation of the information they provided.

6) Change behavior: Lastly, propose your solution. Strategically present your idea and articulate how your support (and possibly others) will promote a successful outcome. Talk about the future, paint a picture of your way-forward plan, and walk the speaker through the process.

You are now ready for Step five.

CHAPTER FIVE: SEPARATE

Growing up, as competition increased in academics, sports and business my father often said, "At this level all of the dogs can hunt." I repeated that quote to myself many times over the years, especially as my career escalated into management. The meaning behind the quote was that at a particular level everyone has the ability to accomplish the mission.

The difference maker lies in who can do it the best and most efficiently. For example, all Major League Baseball pitchers must be able to perform at a high level to remain in the league; however, only a few of them are considered great. This is because only a handful can separate their abilities from their peers and competitors. They are uniquely better at throwing certain pitches (i.e. accuracy, velocity, mechanics), managing their game plans, and handling stress. Those who can perform the best stand out.

The second part to the quote relates to "political influence." In every organization there are office politics. These are actions or behaviors in the workplace that can influence management decisions and create additional competition. Having political influence can also help you separate yourself from others in the same niche. One way to acquire this is to identify and step into opportunities that allow you to expose your abilities to the right audience.

This audience includes key decision makers. For example, as a senior manager I recognized and voluntarily stepped into opportunities that allowed me to lead a high-profile project or operation. These types of assignments required routine updates to executive leaders. They were also infrequent and offered an equal value of reward or risk. The reward was that if I led successfully the executive leaders would see I was reliable and could get things done effectively.

This would pay dividends down the road towards consideration of promotion opportunities. The risk was if I was unsuccessful or not as efficient as they expected, then the executive leaders would also see that and it could negatively affect my reputation and ability to promote. Personally, I never expected to fail and jumped at the opportunities to shine a light on my leadership abilities. Best said by Roman philosopher Seneca, "Luck is what happens when preparation meets opportunity."

Your confidence in your own abilities should overshadow your doubts. The fear of failure is not a valid reason to refrain from taking calculated risks that offer substantial rewards.

Shortly after moving into a new management position, I surrounded myself with smart and talented people (as much as I could early on), listened to my team and asked how can we improve operations and administrative adherence. I visually and verbally provided a clear understanding of the behavior needed to achieve the mission, then intensely looked outwardly across my competitors and colleagues at the same level. I noted areas where I could separate the way I do business from others and asked myself what I could do to be better.

Sometimes it was as simple as altering how I prepared for a meeting or established a new administrative channel to streamline an operational need. While at other times it was more complicated and involved a structural change to a specific line of business. In any case, identifying ways to increase efficiency, standout, and separate from the pack is critical and helps bring successful habits.

Here are ways to start your separation as a mid-level manager or higher.

First, recognize at least one aspect of your personal routine that can be altered to make you better. This includes changing your start time to allow yourself more opportunities to be productive. In today's world technology allows us to communicate and be more accessible than ever before. However, many people do a terrible job of managing those communications. It simply overwhelms them and they often become non-responsive to important emails and text messages.

Review your communication management strategy and determine whether you are as responsive as you should be across all communication platforms. Rule of thumb, all business-related emails and text messages should be answered within four hours. That is a very generous timeframe. I make it a point to respond well within one hour. Even if you simply reply "Received," and respond in more details when able. A lack of or delayed response is unprofessional and leads the sender to believe you are not as engaged as you should be, or simply cannot manage multiple tasks.

Another aspect of communication to review is how you can better cascade important messages to your team. This can help both increase morale and open communication channels. Are your messages clear, concise and timely? Have you asked your team for feedback on your communication style? Leaders who are strong public speakers are often portrayed as being more effective. Sharpen your ability to communicate both verbally and non-verbally.

Secondly, task your team supervisors to identify and articulate better practices in their departments. You are looking for areas that help open your visibility. If their answers are "there are none," then your response should include ideas similar to the steps you are taking to strengthen your own inefficiencies. By positively changing the practices of those around you it will in turn aid in your ability to make well-informed decisions.

Thirdly, review your core administrative processes. You're not aiming to reinvent as much as you are working to streamline. Are there any areas here where you can better your employee, client, or vendor experience? For example, are quarterly business reviews (QBRs) being conducted on time? If so, is the content meaningful or is there room to improve the agendas?

Another element in the administrative process to focus on: How is important information being escalated to those who need to know it? Are you and your fellow leaders receiving timely, concise notifications? Set a framework or protocol that clearly lists what types of matters need to be escalated, and exactly how those escalations are to be communicated. For example, the situation, action, background (SAB) format is popularly used and covers critical areas needed for high-level briefings. These can be concise emails sent forward to relay matters that fall within your escalation protocol. More sensitive matters may require verbal notifications. Ensure that up-to-date phone trees are in place so the right employees can be notified of matters that need their attention.

Fourth, examine your employee lifecycle management process. Do you have the resources in place to continue to recruit talent? Are you diversifying your team to represent today's society? This is important. Tomorrow's leaders should be drawn from your most talented pool of employees who represent an array of races and religions from each gender.

Many companies today have executive leadership teams that do not include any minorities. The glaring problem there is that these companies are handcuffing their ability to truly understand their consumers, customers and clients' needs; especially, if they are attempting to operate on a national or global scale. If your executive leadership team does not remotely represent the society it aims to target, then they are likely knowingly or unknowingly losing ground.

Talk with your Human Resource Department leaders, be an active part of the strategic recruitment plan, and understand how their actions are aligning with the overall direction/mission of the organization.

Fifth, review the core function of your organization. For most this is operations, production and/or manufacturing. For law enforcement and the military it may be threat prioritization. Examine how the core function of the business is running and have honest discussions with line level operators to determine how things can be done more effectively.

A common mistake leaders make is changing or reorganizing a key component or process without first seeking valuable input from those directly affected. As simple as that sounds, it is continuously overlooked. After your review and frank discussions, meet again with mid-level operational and finance managers to ensure the proposed solution or adjustment is advantageous to both your people and your targeted forecast. Be sure to include your information technology (IT) team members in these discussions. In today's public and private environments technological solutions are often the most efficient.

Tips to help you separate you and your business from others:

1) Know your market: Intimately know your competitors and customers. Research customer needs and forecast what that need may look like five years from now. Instead of riding the market, aim to drive the market. Study your closest competitors and review their profitability or EBITDA (earnings before interest, taxes, depreciation and amortization). This will help you better make critical decisions that affect profit margins and help differentiate your product and/or service from others in the same lines of business.

2) Invest in better customer service: After living and working in Asia, for several years it is difficult for me to understand how some U.S. and European businesses can even compete in the area of customer service. Korean Airlines is an excellent example. Compare the customer service they provide with any U.S. airline, and you will find Korean Airlines is light years ahead.

It is not just a cultural difference, but an intense understanding of the subject through education and implementation. The separation they exude in this area is remarkable. Invest a respectable amount of resources aimed at developing and bettering your customer service. As a result, your ROI will be the enhancement of your brand and reputation.

3) Learn from the mistakes of others: Prior to implementing a new administrative procedure, streamlining a workflow process, or launching a new vertical (line of business), take time to research its effectiveness. Talk with peers and review materials online to find out how others failed at doing the same or similar moves. Use that information to your advantage to help ensure that you do not make the same mistakes.

4) Be innovative: Ask questions and drill down on specific and low cost ways to become more

effective in certain areas. Eliminate inconveniences and provide new ideas that resolve known issues. Eliminate an area or areas that do not bring revenue or lack a respectable ROI. Schedule mandatory "think-tank" sessions with managers to draw and capture new and innovative ideas in areas they know best. Use these ideas to assess and target new clients, and work with your sales teams to activate these ideas into their messaging strategies.

5) Be relentless: Never stop moving forward. CEO Tim S. Grover said it best, "Crave the result so intensely that the work is irrelevant." Instill that mindset and live by it. When outside challenges pull you away from complete focus, find time to reset and realign into a state of relentlessness. I say, "It is the drive that gets you to the destination, not the ride."

Next is Step six.

CHAPTER SIX: EVALUATE

Once you have made the appropriate adjustments and changes to separate you and your team apart from others, allow time for the processes to be fully implemented. This provides ample time for managers and employees to get accustomed and determine if the new changes are resulting in their projected outcomes. Next, evaluate these adjustments and verify that they are best suited. The evaluation step is important and should be focused on yourself, your team, your organization as a whole, and how it now stacks up to your competitors.

Start with yourself. Have you clearly communicated the organization's vision and goals to your people? What more can you do to provide them with the tools they need to be even more effective? Communication strategies can easily be reviewed and pushed forward; however, there may be financial constraints that do not allow for additional employee resources. Take this into account and set new attainable goals for yourself to help acquire additional training tools, if needed.

Revisit the culture of the workforce through your interactions with employees at all levels and determine if the high level of work ethic that you patented remains. If not, what can you do to change that? In law enforcement, officers and agents can lose their lives when they become complacent. In that field they often say, "complacency kills" and unfortunately the examples are endless.

In leadership across all sectors, complacency leads to stagnation which kills change and ultimately innovation and profit. Do not become complacent. Ask yourself what you can do to continue to make yourself a better leader for you and your organization.

Assess your executive and mid-level leaders. Focus at these levels because great employees leave bad managers. You must ensure that your leadership teams are effective, or you jeopardize losing the valued talent that you worked hard to recruit and develop.

Is your leadership team passionate about achieving their identified goals and objectives? Does statistical data support that answer? Do their departments reflect favorable quarterly budget forecasts and actuals? Are they providing you with the information that you need to make decisions? Meaning, are you getting above-adequate feedback that aligns with performance?

Tie in your assessment with take-aways for yourself that relate back to what you can do to help make your leadership team better in each of these areas. This assessment does not need to be a formal process. You can construct surveys or simply schedule one-on-one meetings with each of them and have frank discussions. Remember the importance of speaking truth to power.

That philosophy works both ways and during these conversations you want to leverage your ability to constructively coach on areas that you need changed. Setting the appropriate relationship early on will greatly determine your ability to change behavior at this stage.

To simplify the process of assessing the organization as a whole and allow for it to be done sufficiently and without outsourcing, I have broken it down into three key areas.

1) Culture: Review the office culture and employee morale. Depending on the size of the organization a carefully constructed survey is likely the most ideal method to capture culture and overall morale. There are many of these on the market that are inexpensive, can be easily applied online to a large workforce, and calculated into a digestible format that provides useful feedback.

Office culture and employee morale impact productivity and leaders must pay close attention to their employees' needs, or they will pay for it in other areas that affect profit margins. Pay close attention to results related to supervisory support, compensation packages and rewards, branding, training, and growth. Below are two tools to help boost morale and enhance office culture.

Town Halls - Communicate key messages with your executive leaders directly to employees. Allow them to hear input across departments, explain the impact on them and how it moves towards the company's mission. Keep the topics specific, present new material, and vary your delivery platform on each occasion.

Host an employee outing - Nothing builds team unity more than getting employees together at various levels, out of the office, and engaging them in an out-of-the-box activity that requires teamwork to complete a shared goal. These events provide mental health breaks for employees and can result in increased productivity. Furthermore, they allow leaders to learn more about the talents of their team members.

2) Finances: Alongside your Chief Financial Officer (CFO) drill into the financial statements and obtain a holistic view of the company's financial status. Specifically, for many companies, that means review profitability, liquidity and solvency. Determine the areas of operation where revenues are growing and consider sustainability where they are not. Evaluate the financial impact of risks and use that information to drive new ideas, bring on new clients, and/or expand product/service lines.

3) Goals and Objectives: Review department goals and objectives. Each year your leadership team

sets goals to drive attainable achievements. These markers are instrumental in guiding decisions that affect all aspects of the organization. Many times the ability to accomplish these goals are directly tied to employee bonuses in a "pay for performance" type of atmosphere.

Construct a small team of employees drawn from multiple departments to review each goal and confirm whether or not they have successfully been achieved and accurately tie into the overall mission/strategy. If they have, develop new and expanding goals to piggyback off of those accomplished. If not, task your leadership teams to explain and refine the goals with detailed clear instructions of their plans and strategies to achieve them.

Review those with other relevant department leaders to determine how their areas can help to attain these goals. Consider joint goals with cross-functional objectives to foster teamwork in departments currently unaligned. Each goal needs to conform and build into the organization's overall mission. A thorough review of each leader's goals should be conducted at mid-term and at the end of the year. These reviews will provide a blue-print towards reaching your overarching operational strategies, which in turn should positively impact profitability.

After a complete evaluation you are ready for Step seven.

CHAPTER SEVEN: REPEAT

Repeat Steps two through six. Stay engaged and focused on your pursuit of excellence. Continue the "L-Model" loop to sustain effective leadership.

CONCLUSION

The "L-Model" presents a continuously rotating six-step method to learning and maintaining effective leadership. You now have the necessary tools to start or be even more prepared for your journey. By applying what you have learned you have a visual example of at least one leadership style that best aligns with the direction that you want to take your organization. You are able to identify key talent and surround yourself with a team of trusted individuals who are focused on achieving an overall shared mission.

Through personal examples, you can provide your workforce with a new baseline that radiates a culture of hard work. This will standardize employee expectations that meet and exceed a higher level of productivity. This step alone will change the direction of the organization and help to achieve goals and objectives.

Furthermore, you now understand the importance of actively listening, and how to use this skill to motivate people to provide you with information that helps you be better informed to make tough decisions. You know how to create space from your competitors and peers by fostering innovative ideas and implementing changes in areas that streamline, eliminate, or fine tune current administrative and operational methods.

Lastly, you learned the key areas to evaluate to confirm that your changes and leadership decisions have met expectations and are positively impacting operations/productivity, finances and human capital.

The "L-Model" is succinct, accurate, and an outstanding method that brings the reader a proven path to being an effective and successful leader.

- Charles Ayden

Thank you again for purchasing this book!

I hope this book was able to help you to become a more effective leader. The next thing for you to do is to apply the steps you have learned. Please email at CharlesAyden2019@gmail.com to learn more about my other books and online classes! I also welcome your feedback.

www.ingramcontent.com/pod-product-compliance
Lightning Source LLC
Chambersburg PA
CBHW030735180526
45157CB00008BA/3182